Gerd Lu

P9-AFY-684

2/98

The Bernese and Other Mountain Dogs

Bernese, Greater Swiss, Appenzeller, and Entlebucher

Everything about purchase, care, nutrition, breeding, behavior, and training

With 40 color photographs by Christine Steimer

Drawings by György Jankovics

Translated from the German by Elizabeth D. Crawford

BARRON'S

Contents

Inside front cover: A prime example of a Bernese mountain dog. A long daily walk is a must to make sure it gets enough exercise.

Playing by itself, the young dog learns what its body can do.

Preface

Whether it's a Bernese, Greater Swiss, Entlebucher, or Appenzeller, each member of the "Swiss mountain quartet" has its own, unmistakable personality. One thing goes for all four, however: their placid, friendly temperament makes them ideal family dogs. But mountain dogs most certainly are not homebody types. They're always looking for a job to do; they want to be busy and challenged.

This Barron's Pet Owner's Manual presents all four Swiss mountain dog breeds: the Entlebucher as the smallest family member, the impressive Greater Swiss, the restless Appenzeller, and the good-natured Bernese, with comprehensive information about appearance, size and weight, coat and color, temperament, maintenance, grooming, and typical breed characteristics of each.

The HOW-TO pages provide you with valuable tips on training, grooming, feeding, and health maintenance. The book covers everything from buying a puppy to breeding, taking into account the special requirements of each breed. In addition, there are exercise programs you can use to keep your dog fit.

This pet manual is indispensable for anyone who wants to understand his or her mountain dog and care for it properly.

The author and the editors wish you a lot of fun with your mountain dog.

History of Swiss Mountain Dogs

Origins of the Mountain Dogs

To discover the origins of the four Swiss mountain dog breeds, the Bernese, the Appenzeller, Entlebucher, and Greater Swiss (or Swissy), it is necessary to turn the clock back nearly one hundred years and go searching in the remote alpine valleys of Switzerland, just like the geologist Albert Heim. It would be perfectly correct to label the Zurich professor "the father of the mountain dog." Without him, there might not be any breeding line of the four recognized breeds left today.

The professor's great service is that he recognized in the "colored dogs" of the alpine farmers, herdsmen, and butchers the valuable legacy of an old, hardworking dog breed with steadfast temperament. Thanks to the outstanding reputation he enjoyed as a scientist, he was also able to get his convictions and breeding ideas accepted.

Until the turn of the century, even in Switzerland, there was no talk of developing a breed of Swiss mountain dogs. Little wonder, for only the well-to-do could keep a dog for pleasure and were willing and able to undertake the expense of feeding, say, a trained hunting dog. Farmers, workmen, and tradesmen had of course kept dogs since time immemorial. But these simply belonged to the inventory of the house and farm and made themselves useful as watchdogs, herders, and draft dogs. Furthermore, no one ever thought of paying a penny for such an animal. Nevertheless people knew about the

This Entlebucher is howling because he feels he's been left all alone.

virtues of particular temperamental and physical characteristics, were mindful of desirable genetic traits of the parent animals when breeding, and took pains—necessarily without modern knowledge of animal psychology—to provide intelligent education and training of the dog. The measure of all things was ability and usefulness: as drovers of cattle, as reliable protectors of property, or as strong-as-a-bear dray dogs harnessed to loaded dogcarts. No one tolerated useless mouths to feed.

From Worker to Status Symbol

Heim, Schertenleib, Siber, and Strebel were the names of those early fanciers. Over many years they tirelessly searched in all the cantons of Switzerland for suitable breeding dogs that conformed to their ideas of the new breed, set out the breeding goals, and organized the first mountain dog shows. It's only fair, too, to mention the name of Heinrich Schumacher, the master butcher from Bern, who established the modern Saint Bernard breed. The Saint Bernard isn't actually one of the mountain dog breeds, of course; but its close relationship to the Greater Swiss is undeniable.

Today there are more than 400 dog breeds worldwide. Among dog lovers, the mountain dogs are unarguably considered some of the most beautiful. The Bernese is the foremost of all four dog breeds. The aura of the stately dog with its lively dark brown eyes, glossy black coat on its back, glowing bright

The Swissy in its original home, Switzerland.

brown patches, and broad, pure white chest of course also adds cachet to any owner. Therefore the Bernese, in particular, has advanced to the status of fashionable pet. Unfortunately, it isn't unusual for many a mountain dog to have to suffer as a decorative ornament to a villa or country house. There's nothing more absurd you could do to it. For under its magnificent exterior there hides a real workaholic, both by heredity and temperament, a dog that loves nothing more than to be challenged by work and duties. Its alpine relatives, the Greater Swiss, the Appenzeller, and Entlebucher, are not one bit different. None of the four mountain dog breeds are born for lolling at home among the sofa cushions. They are constantly looking for occupation and challenge. Anyone who flirts with the idea of owing a Swiss mountain dog had better have this firmly in mind beforehand. Those who neglect this criterion for ownership will only too quickly produce an unstable grouch and a notorious good-for-nothing (see Mountain Dogs Need Work, page 36).

Comparing the Mountain Dogs

The alpine four may have a great deal in common in heredity and looks, but today, thanks to deliberate, careful breeding, each of the four has developed its own utterly unmistakable personality. All new mountain dog admirers are able to choose among the four breeds for their own personal companion. Although two of the breeds are already available in the United States, it takes a little more determination to want an overseas representative of one of the other two breeds.

The Bernese yields nothing to the other mountain dog breeds in versatility and family usefulness. Its original sphere of work as watch dog and herd and draft dog on the farm still define its temperament and character. Today its good qualities as an easily directed working dog make it perfectly suited for partnership in the family. The Bernese mountain dog is absolutely the first choice for a reliable friend and protector of children, a guardian for the whole family, and an agreeable companion. The Bernese is the only one of the four mountain dogs that is fully recognized by the American Kennel Club (AKC) (see address, page 62).

The Greater Swiss owes its breed's existence entirely to the expert eye of Professor Heim, who, as the judge at a Bernese show, was confronted with a dog that was a marvelous, imposing specimen but that had short hair. The impressive fellow was undiminished even when surrounded by the long-haired Bernese mountain dogs. Albert Heim spotted this immediately. But he also recollected the sturdy butcher's dogs that he'd observed in different places in Switzerland several years previously, and he dubbed the extraordinary show dog a Greater Swiss. The year was 1908, the year of the birth of the Greater Swiss mountain dog. In their character and appearance, the Greater Swiss and the Saint Bernard show their common past utterly unmistakably, especially if you look at the original Saint Bernard dogs in old photos or drawings. Its long muzzle and flatter skull, today no longer typical of the breed, are astonishingly reminiscent of the large butcher's dog or mountain dog. Again, in other pictures of long-haired Saint Bernards with dark backs, their closeness to Bernese mountain dogs is apparent.

In terms of relationship, Appenzellers and Entlebuchers are further removed from the Bernese and the Greater Swiss than the Saint Bernard is. However, there's a simple, prosaic reason for the continued maintenance of the Saint Bernard as an independent breed: it had nothing in common with the cattle dogs and watchdogs of the farmers and "little" people, but by the middle of the previous century was already a sought-after token of luxury. Possession of a Saint Bernard was reserved solely for the well-to-do, especially if one of the few really pure-bred animals was involved. Naturally a Saint Bernard didn't have to pursue a regular occupation like the common mountain dog.

In the United States, the Greater Swiss is lovingly called "Swissy" by all who know this breed. The first Swissy was born in this country in 1970. In 1985, the breed was admitted to the American Kennel Club's Miscellaneous List. This means that the process is underway to get the Swissy fully registered.

The Appenzeller, was and is for all intents and purposes a utility dog. It's lively, extraordinarily persistent, an outstanding herder and watchdog, yet easily pleased and eager to learn. Just under medium size, with short hair, this mountain dog's distinguishing characteristic is its "post-horn" tail, curled in a ring and carried to the side. In the early years of the breed, when the line between the Appenzeller and its near relative the Entlebucher was fluid, its tail often was just like the other's. For the modern Appenzeller the curl is the standard and, together with its roguish-friendly facial expression, clearly provides it with a bonus of appeal.

The Entlebucher isn't in any way inferior to the Appenzeller when it comes to usefulness, although sometimes it's hard to believe this of the smallest of the four mountain dog breeds—a mistake, as fanciers of the breed continually stress. This self-assured, fidgety, well-muscled package of power is a "terrific guy." It's reasonable to assume that this relatively easy-to-keep breed may still come into its own. Becoming rare, the dogs are still employed in Switzerland today in military and emergency services.

Note: One pages 12 to 19 you'll find a detailed description of the individual mountain dog breeds.

Playing is fun, and even more so with another dog. The Swissy (right) in a typical position of expectation.

Typical Mountain Dogs

Swiss mountain dogs are "sturdy types" in the truest sense of the word. This characterization applies not just to their sturdy build, but to their "two-fisted," reliable, uncomplicated nature as well.

Herding and Guarding

Mountain dogs have both herding and guarding in their blood. Most no longer show direct evidence of it today, except for the few who help the alpine herdsmen and other alp dwellers with their work. Nevertheless, you can surmise it on the basis of the behavior patterns the mountain dog exhibits in its family; for example, our family's Sunday walk with our four-year-old Bernese Tami. As long as we walkers form a closed unit, everything's all right with Tami. But if someone falls behind, her hereditary virtues emerge: she circles the group constantly and runs from one to the other, her tail lifted in command. There's no peace until we're all back together again.

With the two smaller mountain dog breeds, Appenzeller and Entlebucher, the protective instinct—protecting and herding necessarily complement each other—is even more pronounced.

Herding cattle was the most important duty of every mountain dog for many generations. Also, though the dogs were not yet bred to standards, farmers preferred to mate their herding champions with each other. This legacy is deeply rooted in the modern, usually nonworking, family mountain dog. It's estimated that over 90 percent of Appenzeller and Entlebucher puppies are born with these characteristics or at least have a tendency toward them. The figure is somewhat smaller for the Greater Swiss and Bernese. Cutting out and encircling animals and people is an essential part of the normal developmental behavior of mountain dog puppies, as is playfully heel-biting every real and putative herding object. This is how the adult Appenzeller adds reinforcing effect to its strenuous job, by "spurring" as it runs after the cattle (see drawing, page 10). Although it often controls the herd entrusted to it by yelping in their ears, a Greater Swiss carries out its job almost soundlessly.

Independent Action

A typical character trait of the mountain dog is its ability to act on its own. This is a must for a perfect herd dog, so it will be a reliable partner on the job. It usually grasps the situation very much faster than any herdsman and acts accordingly. Thus a good Appenzeller easily replaces two or three herd boys.

Therefore anyone looking for a four-legged companion that hangs with doggish loyalty on the word and gestures of its master is making a mistake with a mountain dog. For all their great love for their family, mountain dogs are not cringers and mere order takers. Rather, they are dependable and understanding partners. Accordingly, their training should be gentle, without drill sergeant behavior and loud commands, but absolutely consistent and firm.

The Entlebucher loves to take a bath in the lake.

Guarding and Protective Instincts

These dogs definitely belong to an inherited program of guarding behaviors. Mountain dogs are the most devoted guardians you can imagine. An infant will grow up perfectly secure, especially under the protection of either of the two large breeds, the Bernese and the Swissy. The mountain dog takes over protecting and, if necessary, defending the house and

On land again, its coat gets a good shaking.

grounds without being asked. In addition, you can ask it to protect specific objects at any time.

Take advantage of this trait when your darling is left home alone against its will and demonstrates during your absence with loud expressions of disapproval or a little vandalism. The immobilizing trick: Before leaving the house, give the dog an object to watch—preferably things that remind it of its master, for instance a briefcase or some old trousers. As a proud guardian with a special duty, it is now able to give up its wicked pleasures every time, not just the first time (see Give the Dog Jobs, page 37).

Guarding a Herd

To a nonworking mountain dog, guarding a herd means the guarding of its human family. It feels in its element when its entire human flock surrounds it. Our Tami obviously counts the heads of her loved ones every evening. She's only satisfied when the last one gets home. Therefore we must classify the mountain dog as a multiperson dog by nature. This is another relic of a farm dog past. The farmer could seldom spend much time with the dog. The dog belonged to the farm and to the family. It was imperative that it trust all equally and obey all. Naturally an Entlebucher or Appenzeller today is happy in a single-person household; nevertheless, its true happiness is still the family. It's obvious, by the way, that for a dog that always lives with animals—large or small—there's no question about harmonious partnership with all other animals and pets (see drawing, page 22).

Even the Multitalented Need Training

Awareness of the mountain dog's innate all-around capabilities frequently leads to the supposition that the puppies are born already "schooled." This is a false and dangerous notion, because it can lead to the young puppy's not receiving the necessary training. With proper training, a mountain dog is an astonishingly multitalented animal and is also generally useful as a utility dog: from rescue and avalanche worker to guardian and Seeing-Eye dog.

Herding cattle, the Appenzeller reinforces its directions with the typical nipping at the heels ("spurring").

10

A Short Glossary

Here are some technical terms you should know if you're interested in mountain dogs.

Blaze: The red or glossy rust-red color of a dog's coat is referred to as blaze. Not least, the brilliant red on the head, sides of the chest, and legs make the mountain dog unmistakable.

Double coat: With the exception of the Bernese's long coat, the double coat is typical for the mountain dog. It consists of the thick undercoat and the medium-length outer coat, is cold- and water-resistant, and at the same time is absolutely easy care.

Draft work: With dogcarts and special harnesses, the Bernese and the Greater Swiss can pull very heavy loads. Today, in country districts in Switzerland, milk and other farm products are still transported by dog team (see page 37).

Fetching: Bringing objects, either on command or voluntarily, is especially pronounced with the Entlebucher and the Appenzeller. Besides herding and guarding, fetching is a clear expression of mountain dogs' uncontrollable need to work (see page 37).

Herding and guarding: The protective instinct is considered the most noticeable character trait of the mountain dog. The heritage of their farm dog ancestors, selected for their herding and guarding abilities, is very active in all four breeds.

Hip dysplasia: Unfortunately, hip problems are reported in all Swiss mountain dogs. Hip dysplasia (HD) leads to deformities, such as degener-ation of the joint. It is an inherited disease, primarily in large dog breeds (see page 53).

Ring tails and docked tails: In the Appenzeller, the ring tail carried to one side, the little post horn, is an unmistakable breed characteristic. The tail of the Entlebucher is usually the result of docking, though in rare instances puppies are born with short tails.

Selection: In Europe only selected purebred dogs receive permission for breeding. Appearance and temperament are the basis of selection. Thus, the breeding association makes sure that only an animal that conforms to the standard will pass on its genes (see page 56). In the United States, the responsibility for breeder selection is left to the breeder.

Temperament: Despite individual differences, there are typical features of temperament in different dog breeds. Just like body build, coat structure, and markings and color, temperament is the result of domestication and purposeful breeding choices. In the mountain dog breeds, their capacity for independent action, marked desire for partnership with humans and animals, need for close attachment to a family structure, and their great perceptiveness are all striking.

Tricolor: Characteristic markings of the four Swiss mountain dogs are the tricolored coats with dark back, white on the head, chest, and toes as well as glossy rust-red (see Blaze, above). Its (ideally) symmetrical markings and strong coloration make the mountain dog coat look very attractive.

The puppy is already able to growl when someone tries to take a toy away from it.

A long, silky coat is typical for the Bernese. Black is the only background color permitted in tricolored coats.

The Bernese

It's a family dog made to measure: good-natured, very affectionate, alert, and fearless in any situation. On the other hand, with strangers it acts friendly and self-confident but aloof. A strong dog, who appreciates long walks. For a detailed portrait, see page 14.

This Bernese has even the white at the tip of the tail that is desirable according to the standard.

The Entlebucher

Wit and impishness are written in its face. Along with all its keenness and independence, it seeks closeness to "its" people. It will even overlook some mistakes in training. For a detailed portrait, see page 15.

The young dogs play all day long until they almost fall over with weariness.

The Entlebucher's double coat is typical for its breed: short, firm shining top hair coat with thicker furlike undercoat.

Portrait of the Bernese

The Bernese is named for its place of origin, the Bernese uplands.

AKC Standard for the Bernese Mountain Dog

General appearance: The Bernese is a striking, tricolored, large dog that is sturdy and balanced. It is intelligent, strong, and agile. Males appear masculine; females, distinctly feminine.

Size, proportion, substance: Males are 25 to 27.5 inches (63.5–70 cm) at the withers. Though squarish, the Bernese is slightly longer than tall. The body is full, the bones sturdy.

Head: The *expression* is intelligent, animated, gentle. The *eyes* are dark brown, oval, with close-fitting eyelids. The *ears* are mid-sized, triangular, with gently rounded tips. Set level with the top of the skull, they hang close to the head when in repose, are brought forward and raised at the base when the dog is alert. The *skull* is flat, broad, with a slight furrow and well-defined stop. The *muzzle* is strong, straight. The *nose* is black. The *lips* are clean, the *mouth* dry, the *flews* only slightly developed. *Dentition* is complete; the *teeth* meet in a scissors bite.

Neck, topline, body: The *neck* is strong, muscular, medium-length. The *topline* is level from the withers to the croup. The *chest* is deep, capacious, with well-sprung ribs and brisket reaching to at least the elbows. The *back* is broad, firm. The *loin* is strong. The *croup* is broad, rounded. The *tail* is bushy, carried low in repose; an upward swirl is permissible when the dog is alert. The tail bones should feel straight and reach to the hock joint or below.

Forequarters: The shoulders are moderately laid back, flat-lying, well-muscled, never loose. The *legs* are straight, strong; the *elbows* are well under the shoulder when the dog is standing. The *pasterns* slope very slightly, are never weak. The *feet* are round, compact, with well-arched toes. The *dewclaws* may be removed.

Hindquarters: The *thighs* are broad, strong, muscular. The *stifles* are moderately bent, tapering into the hocks. The *hocks* are well let down, straight. The *feet* are compact, face forward. The *dewclaws* are removed.

Coat: The *coat* is thick, mid-length, shiny, straight or slightly wavy.

Color, markings: The Bernese is black with rust and white markings. Rust appears over each eye, on the cheeks, on the chest, on all four legs, and under the tail. The blaze is white, as is a muzzle band and the tip of the tail. White on the feet is desired but not higher than the pasterns.

Gait: The natural gait is a slow trot. The reach in front is good. The back is level, transmitting a powerful drive. With speed, the legs tend to converge.

Temperament: The Bernese is self-confident, alert, good-natured, never sharp or shy, sometimes aloof.

Disqualifications: Blue eyes, a ground color other than black.

A Bernese that corresponds to the standard.

Portrait of the Entlebucher

The Entlebucher is the smallest of the Swiss mountain dogs. Throughout Europe it is finding more and more friends, primarily because of its "handy" size and uncomplicated care.

Appearance: Only too often it's called a mongrel or an undersized Bernese with short hair. Its body is somewhat longer than it is high, but it's extremely muscular. Its efficiently angled legs allow a strong, free flow of movement.

Size and weight: Height at the withers is between 15.5 and 19.5 inches (39.4–49.5 cm); weight is 55 to 66 pounds (24.9–29.9 kg).

Coat and color: The hairs of the outer coat are short, firm, and shining and there is a dense undercoat (double coat). Deep black ground color, yellow to rust-brown markings, white on head, chest, and paws. A white semicircular or thinly encircling neck ring is permitted in the standard.

Temperament: The Entlebucher is not only a faithful watchdog and companion; over its long years of service as a cattle herder and drover, it's demonstrated one thing above all: its independence and its ability to size up a situation with lightning speed. Yet, despite all its keenness and independence, it always likes to be near "its" people. It will forgive some mistakes by an inexperienced trainer. Entlebuchers are born optimists, who make sure there's always life in the party. Sometimes they do it quite loudly, admittedly, so you should take pains even with puppies to be sure they don't learn to enjoy yapping. An Entlebucher gets along very well with other animals.

Living conditions: The Entlebucher can be happy in a large city apartment, too, but it needs regular exercise. The inventors of the agility competition, in which the dog and master go through a fitness course (see Agility, page 38), must have been thinking of the Entlebucher when they created this new leisure-time activity. An Entlebucher is almost peerless in its agility and flexibility. It loves to swim in any kind of water.

Grooming: Its short-haired coat should be combed with a flea comb daily and groomed with a natural bristle or rubber curry brush (see HOW-TO, page 43).

Illnesses typical of the breed: Almost a third of all breed lines have to contend with hip dysplasia (HD) of varying degrees of severity (see page 53). But there is cause for hope: With the help of computers and with recent experience, the European mountain dog clubs are now able to furnish their members effective breeding help, identifying animals that are guaranteed free of HD.

Special note: Most Entlebuchers are born with long tails, which are later docked. Josef W. Pohling, president of the Swiss Mountain Dog Club of Germany, says about this: "In the new standard the long tails will have to be allowed." German animal protection laws, much stricter than those in the United States, no longer allow docking.

An Entlebucher that corresponds to the standard.

The Greater Swiss

Its body size gains it respect, its gentle nature makes it an ideal family dog. Physically and mentally, it's an extraordinarily agile and teachable dog. For a detailed portrait, see page 18.

The Swissy has a body that is sturdy but by no means plump, with a strikingly broad chest. These little puppies will one day achieve the stately size of more than 25.5 inches (64.8 cm) at the withers.

The Appenzeller

It bonds closely to its primary person and will go through fire for its master or mistress. On the other hand, with strangers it exhibits unmistakable aloofness. The Appenzeller mountain dog can hardly be restrained in its eagerness to work. A keen, independent dog of action—a dog with amazing perceptive faculties. Unmistakable because of its cheery tail curled in a ring. For a detailed portrait, see page 19.

Like the Entlebucher and the Swissy, the Appenzeller has a double coat consisting of medium-length cover hair and a thick undercoat.

A champion for the books: This Appenzeller has fulfilled all evaluation criteria with highest marks.

Portrait of the Greater Swiss

This stately dog undoubtedly goes back to the Swiss farm and butcher's dogs, whose capacity and willingness to work were what counted.

The Standard of the Greater Swiss Mountain Dog Club of America

General appearance: The Greater Swiss is a large, powerful, alert, short-coated dog of sturdy appearance.

Head: The head is flat and broad, with a slight stop, strong, not clumsy. The skull and muzzle are of equal length. The muzzle is blunt, not pointed, moderately long and power-ful, never snipelike. The nose is broad with a slight rise before the end. All teeth are present, with a scissors bite. The eyes are dark brown, medium size, neither deep-set nor prominent, with tight lids. The ears are of medium size, triangular, set fairly high and hanging flat, but carried forward when the dog is alert. Tight, clean lips without flaws. No dewlap.

Neck and body: The neck is medium length, strong, muscular, clean. Body length to height is 10 to 9. The back is moderately long, strong, straight. The belly is straight. The chest is deep, broad, with a slightly protruding breastbone. The ribs are well sprung. The withers is high, long. The loins are broad, powerful. The croup is long, broad, slightly rounded. The tail is fairly level, reaching to the hocks. It is carried down in repose, only slightly raised when excited.

A Swissy that corresponds to the breed standard.

Forequarters: The shoulders are long, sloping and strong, flat, well muscled. The forelegs are straight, strong. The feet are round, compact, with long arched toes, strong nails. The dew-claws are removed.

Coat: The top coat is dense, 1 to 1.75 inches (about 2.5–5 cm) The undercoat is thick and sometimes showing.

Color: The coat is shiny black with glossy rust-red marks on the cheeks, above the eyes, and on all four legs. There is a symmetrical white blaze on the muzzle and chest. White is found on the feet and tail tip. A small white patch on the back of the neck or a white ring around the neck is permit-ted. The absence of white on the blaze or chest is a fault. Red always lies between black and white.

Gait: There is good reach in the front, powerful drive from the rear. Movement is with a level back.

Size: Males are 25.5 to 28.5 inches (64.8–72.4 cm) at the shoulder; females are 23.5 to 24 inches (59.7–61 cm).

Temperament: The Swissy is bold, faithful, willing, alert, vigilant.

Disqualifications: Blue eye color, any ground color other than black.

The Swissy has made steady progress since coming to the U.S. in 1968. The Greater Swiss Mountain Dog Club of America has 1,000 Swissys registered. This slow increase due to careful breeding and selection of imports has maintained the high level of soundness and temperament of the breed.

Swissys can be shown in the Miscellaneous Class of the AKC as well as in AKC licensed Obedience Trials and Tracking Tests. In 1992, the Greater Swiss Mountain Dog Club of America began formal application to the AKC for full recognition in the Working Class.

Portrait of the Appenzeller

Formerly the Appenzeller was the quintessential drover's dog. Its impetuous temperament can only be controlled if you give it an adequate workout.

Appearance: The barely medium-sized dog has a muscular body. Characteristic is its short, curled, ring tail, the so-called post horn.

Size and weight: Its height at the withers is between 19 and 22.5 inches (48 and 58 cm); its weight between 61 and 77 pounds (28 to 35 kg).

Coat and color: The Appenzeller has a medium-long outer coat with a thick undercoat (double coat). The ground color may be black or Havana brown. The fur over the eyes, and on the legs, chest, and cheeks is a strong brown-red; there are white markings on the head, throat, chest, and possibly also on the feet and tip of the tail. A white semicircular or thin continuous neck ring is permitted in the standard.

Temperament: It shows reserve with strangers more strongly than its kindred, sometimes even exhibiting open mistrust. But it'll go through fire for its master or mistress. It announces strangers in its relatively high voice—that of the male being usually higher than that of the female—relentlessly and incessantly until its master tells it to stop. The Appenzeller is incredibly quick and almost unrestrainable in its eagerness to work. It is very keen, has an inherited urge to act independently, and possesses amazing perceptive faculties.

Living conditions: The Appenzeller must always have something to do, otherwise its temperament is almost uncontrollable. Offer it challenges as a companion in jogging, walking, with bicycling, or on mountain hikes. It loves boisterous play. The Appenzeller needs consistent and intelligent training and a constant, stable pack relationship. Whereas the Entlebucher will forgive its owner some faults in living conditions or training, the Appenzeller quickly demonstrates who is the real boss. Then its strong drive to guard can become independent, even to the point of viciousness.

It notices the scents of wild animals, but as a rule it scarcely bothers about them. Rather, it watches over its family during walks. The Appenzeller never passes up a chance for a total bath in a lake or a stream.

Grooming: It's enough to comb its coat with the flea comb and brush it with a natural-bristled brush daily (see HOW-TO, page 43).

Illnesses typical of the breed: Appenzeller are robust, little prone to illness, and long-lived. Occasionally animals will grow up oversensitive or timid, which a responsible breeder—and even more the breed club, by withholding permission to breed—will prevent from breeding.

An Appenzeller that corresponds to the breed standard.

Advice on Buying

Long before buying a mountain dog you should be clear about what characteristics you want in your future canine companion, whether you can meet the requirements for keeping an animal, and how ready and able you are to exchange your former dog-free existence for the ongoing responsibility of attending to the needs of the dog.

A Mountain Dog in Your Life?

The following questions should help you make your decision to buy.
1. None of the four mountain dog breeds are suited for living solely in apartments. Can you give a dog enough space and at least offer it a yard?
2. Have you the time to take at least one long walk per day with the dog?
3. Can you spend at least two hours daily with your dog?
4. Can your pet expect a regular daily routine in your family?
5. Does your landlord or condominium association allow in your lease the keeping of large dogs?
6. Can you afford food, grooming, licensing, veterinary, and other costs for the dog? The annual costs are considerable, especially in the first year.
7. Are there people who can look after the dog if you're sick or on vacation?
8. Are all your family members free of allergies to dog hair (see Important Note, page 63)?

Even if you've answered all these questions with "yes," don't forget that your answers must be valid for 10 to 15 years, for on the average, that's how long a well-cared-for mountain dog will live.

Mountain Dogs Are Family Dogs

The four Swiss breeds possess some typical characteristics of temperament that particularly destine them for family living.
• Mountain dogs have a peaceful temperament. They maintain a natural aloofness with strangers and visitors but virtually never display any aggression.
• A well-trained mountain dog is ideal as a responsible, "co-thinking" partner for the whole family.
• Mountain dogs love children. However, be careful about permitting your child to take solo walks with the dog: The strength of the child on the other end of the leash is usually not developed enough for the extraordinary protective instincts of the dog.
• Mountain dogs don't hunt. It does of course happen that an Entlebucher will chase a rabbit for fifty yards, but then the dog has had it.
• Peaceful coexistence is markedly evident. Tolerance toward other animals is a basic requirement for a herd dog. The Swiss mountain dogs don't have to be trained to live in peace with other house pets and animals.
• The bond to house and grounds is so strong in all four breeds that strays have rarity value.

What Mountain Dogs Don't Like
Of course mountain dogs love an

Although the Bernese mountain dog loves to run, it's still not an athlete for endurance or competitive trials. The dog is only fit for endurance runs beside a bicycle after special training—but not in warm weather, because its thick, long coat may cause overheating.

The Bernese needs an extensive walk every day.

easy course of fitness training, but they are less suited for record sprints and endurance runs. The Bernese and the Appenzeller are equally unsuited for a family that only comes together irregularly. Mountain dogs prize nothing more than knowing that "their" people are nearby. There are arguments in the best of families. However, people who are always quarreling will cause great psychological damage to a mountain dog (see page 52).

Male or Female Dog?

Whether you acquire a male or a female depends on your personal preference; basically there's scarcely any difference in temperament. But of course there are gender-specific differences:

The female will come into season twice yearly, in spring and fall (see Breeding, page 58). If you want to avoid having puppies, you have to watch very closely at these times to be sure that a "suitor" doesn't find some way to get a chance to mate. Another means of protection is spaying, which, according to generally accepted opinion, does not result in any psychological changes in the female.

With males the persistent hankering after the "hot" female during walks can degenerate into a test of nerves for the owner. The dog stops at every possible opportunity and lifts his leg to leave his scent marking behind.

Puppy or Full-Grown Dog?

In principle, Swiss mountain dogs are best acquired as puppies. After the age of 16 months, at the very latest, a change of primary person is no longer advisable. The Bernese, for instance, has difficulty coping with a change of owners later in life. It can then become rebellious, disobedient, overanxious, or even vicious.

It goes without saying that you should buy mountain dog puppies exclusively from a recognized breeder. And then you have to summon up some patience. It may be a whole year before you can get a puppy!

Grown dog: Anyone who falls in love with a mountain dog at the animal shelter must have a thorough knowledge of how to keep dogs or else turn the dog over to an experienced trainer (see Important Note, page 63).

For mountain dogs, living together in harmony with other domestic animals and pets is no problem.

22

How You Find the Right Breeder

Buy a mountain dog puppy from a breeder. You can get the addresses of breeders with puppies for sale from Swiss Mountain Dog Clubs located in the United States and in Germany. If you are not sure how to find them contact the American Kennel Club. (See Useful Addresses, page 62.) Through compliance with the breeding guidelines, these breeders guarantee healthy, properly raised animals. When choosing a breeder, observe the following:

1. After deciding which particular mountain dog breed you want, choose as many breeders as you can locate in your region or state, with the goal of visiting those who have or will have pups or adult dogs available.

2. The breeder's dogs should have access to the family and not live in the kennel most of the time. None of the four mountain dog breeds are suited for kennel living.

3. The whelping area of the bitch, the place where the animals live, the bedding, and all food and water dishes must be clean. Are the dogs protected from drafts, dampness, and cold?

4. Avoid any breeder who won't allow you access to the puppies from the third week on after birth. Your puppy must get used to you.

5. The breeder must give you a pedigree, health and immunization certificates, as well as the sales contract.

6. The sales contract should include a return clause in case, contrary to expectation, serious problems occur with the young dog.

7. A good breeder will volunteer to give you support in all the difficulties of daily dealing with the new dog, without your having to ask.

How You Get the Puppy You Want

Whenever possible, a puppy should be bought through a personal visit to the breeder. From the third week after birth until the puppy is given up—usually at ten weeks—you should be with it once a week so that it can get used to you.

The healthy puppy has:
- A round little belly. Caved-in flanks are a reason to worry.
- A glossy, thick coat.
- Clear eyes, no inflammation.
- Clean ears, not sticky.

The temperament of the puppy should also be checked out. The puppy must not seem apathetic.

- The go-getter is the first one at Mama's nipple, the most courageous in exploring the unknown world around the whelping box, the most inquisitive in contact with strangers. Usually this cheeky little devil develops into the so-called alpha animal, self-confident and strong. These dogs need a consistent owner.
- The cautious one quietly observes everything with great interest from the basket's far corner.
- The phlegmatic one concerns itself with eating regularly and sleeping. It prefers to leave strenuous play to others.

Therefore, if you would rather have it easier, you should choose the gentle, quieter puppies that may not grow up to be super champions but nevertheless give reliable love and affection without stirring up a riot.

Getting the Puppy to Feel at Home

It can only be guessed at how painful the separation from mother and siblings is for the puppy. Still, the first tender bonds of trust have already been established between you and the puppy through your visits to the breeder. That helps a bit to mitigate its great distress.

Bringing the Puppy Home

As a rule, it's better to get the puppy by car, with a second person along.

This works well: The passenger takes the little one on his or her lap, strokes it, and speaks softly to it. A towel or blanket under the puppy protects clothing in case it has to vomit. Paper towels should be within easy reach, for all too often the puppy has a small "accident" out of fright. This way there's nothing left to interfere with a secure journey home.

Time to Get Used to the New Home

Everything is already prepared for the arrival of the puppy: basket bed, chewable toys, bowls for water and food (see What Equipment You Need, page 26), the newspaper corner or a cat litter box for the period until the little one is housebroken. What the puppy needs now most of all is peace and quiet, to be able to work through all the exciting and strange impressions and integrate them into its everyday canine life. But if the whole family now coos all over it, reactions of fear and defiance will inevitably surface. During the first 24 hours after the puppy's arrival, your pet should be allowed to sniff around undisturbed, sleep, or simply observe the new world.

The First Night

Place the puppy's basket beside your bed and put an old pair of trousers or a sweater in it. The soon familiar smell of master or mistress signals closeness and security to the scent-oriented dog. It will certainly awaken you several times during this night. Stroke your pet until it falls asleep again. In the course of the day, the puppy will become more self-confident. Then its sleeping basket can be moved to its preestablished place. An old but effective trick can help calm the puppy: Wrap an alarm clock in a hand towel and place the bundle in the puppy's sleeping basket. Clearly, the ticking reminds the puppy of its mother's heartbeat.

No Dog Is Too Young to Learn

Early training shouldn't be neglected if you don't want to have a dog with bad habits later.

Goal 1: Housebreaking. Begin training the puppy to be housebroken even in the very beginning. Basically it means going out after every meal and after every nap. Find it a protected spot and praise your pet as soon as it does anything. At the first signs that the puppy "has to go," it should go right outside (see HOW-TO, page 30). If it happens too fast now and then, don't

Even the laundry hung outdoors is guarded.

punish it. Clean the spot with lemon-scented cleaner or any other cleanser that is currently on the market with the specific purpose of pet odor elimination. The smell, which is unpleasant to the dog's nose, will prevent repetition. Your puppy must be housebroken within 14 days.

Note: In the first few days you can also direct the dog to a cat litter box or a place that has been covered thickly with newspapers. The same principles apply here as above.

The Appenzeller will defend home and turf if necessary.

What Equipment You Need

All the equipment for your dog should be collected before its arrival in your home.

The basket bed means more to the dog than just a place to rest: From here it can look out and observe everything, here it feels hidden and at home. Whether it's a basket or a box, the important thing is a draft-free location on the edge of family activities. Cushions and coverings should be washable. The pet store has attractive sleeping baskets of woven willow in appropriate sizes.

Bowls, one for food and one for water, must be easy to clean. Therefore bowls made of pottery or steel are most suitable. They mustn't tip (broader on the bottom than the top) and should stand securely on a nonskid rubber mat.

As playthings, the most suitable are chewable items made of all rubber or buffalo hide. They don't split, offer playing pleasure over a long period, and at the same time provide the best training for teeth. Metal objects are clearly unsuitable and toys of soft and light plastic are instantly reduced to small pieces by a puppy and may then be swallowed. They have no place in a dog household. Of course there slumbers in every little dog a special pref-

erence for an old shoe and a snuggle blanket. You shouldn't contest its right to the possession, even if it then becomes difficult, because of its previous experience.

The collar for mountain dog puppies can be a simple leather collar for the moment. You then furnish a broad leather collar for the adult mountain dog; these also come with very beautiful mountain dog motifs. You can maintain control over dogs who are incorrigible "draggers" on the leash with a training collar (see drawing, HOW-TO, page 34).

A lead that rolls up makes sense for the dog that is still small. It permits the animal a large radius of movement while being walked. You can keep the leash short or let it roll out to several yards in length. But for the adult mountain dog you need to choose a trustworthy leather lead that isn't too short.

An address tag bearing the name of the dog and its master and the address and telephone number should always be fastened to the dog's collar.

Coat grooming equipment is only an important concern with the Bernese mountain dog. A brush with natural bristles and a coarse comb are part of the basic kit for your pet. With its double-coated and short-haired relatives, the loose hair can be removed by hand or with a rubber curry brush (see page 43).

Goal 2: Good "Table Manners."

Table manners are like learning how to swim: once they're learned, they're learned forever. With a dog, early learning of the boundary between its bowls and your dinner table avoids long, tiresome years of insistent begging and attempted constraint. For the mountain dog, just taking part in the meal of its people is its heart's desire. Being there is enough. Feed the puppy regularly before your own meal and religiously avoid even the tiniest present from the table.

Saying No

High spirits and boisterous play are naturally part of the behavior of a young dog. But the puppy also needs to learn its limits. In a pack, the older animals take over this role. As new leader of the pack, you're responsible for its early socialization.

Anything that you wouldn't allow an adult dog to do in any circumstances should be taboo for the puppy. The puppy in bed? No problem. But will it be the same for a Swissy weighing 110 pounds (50 kg)? Besieging table and bed, tearing and pulling on shoes and clothing, scratching at doors, jumping and licking, begging and biting—seen as youthful behavior, these disruptions are all-too-often allowed to go unpunished. Make it clear to the puppy that you don't go along with this. This isn't about punishment; it's solely about spoiling. Dogs are trained principally by tone of voice; yelling has no role here. However, the young dog learns very quickly to differentiate by the tone of your voice between criticism and praise. Scolding is done with short, sharp words: "No," "Bad," "Stop." However, the effect is only achieved when the puppy is caught in the act. Inevitably, scolding produces a feeling of guilt.

Just as decisive is consistency from everyone in the household! A young dog quickly recognizes "weak spots" in the family, whether it concerns indulgence in behavior or forbidden treats (see training, page 32).

Precautions Don't Hurt

Observe your puppy as carefully and regularly as possible to learn its daily rhythm. Keep track of its appetite, its toilet behavior (including any changes that may occur in its stools), and for at least the first few weeks make a chart of its weight increase (see How Much Food?, page 46, and drawing, page 58). Don't hesitate to call the breeder or to call or visit the veterinarian of your choice if you see changes in the puppy that you can't explain. Its system is still so vulnerable that waiting could be a risk.

Enterprisingly the puppy clambers out of its basket to explore its surroundings.

Understanding Mountain Dogs

The dog has retained many behaviors and characteristics of its ancestors, the wolf. Dog owners must think about this if they want to treat their dog fairly, consistently, and with understanding.

The World Through the Nose

The canine world is one of smells. The dog's most important organ is its nose. In order to get a picture of its environment, a dog needs successive close contact with humans and other members of its species.

When dogs meet, the most important thing is what they can smell. First they sniff nose to nose, then each turns to the other's tail and sniffs the "anal face." Under the tail lie glands that supply completely personal data. From puppyhood on, every dog must have the opportunity to make such contacts to practice getting along peacefully with other dogs.

"Speaking" Doesn't Just Mean Barking

Dogs have a broad range of sounds at their disposal.

Barking is only one of the language patterns. Even here there are many forms of expression, from the light bark inviting play to the watchful warning or the growling angry bark.

Growling is almost always a warning sound.

Howling—inherited from the wolf—is only used in a few situations, for instance when the dog is left alone.

Even a young Swissy knows perfectly well what it may and may not do.

Whimpering and whining is also employed by the adult dog. It is used to express the idea of an appeasing submissive posture or as notice of a pressing need.

Body Language

The body language of dogs also reveals some things about their mood.

Ear signals: Dogs with hanging ears, which all the mountain dog breeds have, are at something of a disadvantage compared to the erect-eared dog breeds when it comes to information value. Nevertheless the heavy, hanging ears can be moved with the help of the ear muscles. If your dog raises its ears, that means alertness. Ears slightly laid back usually signal caution and waiting.

Tail signals: A horizontal tail means contentment. Carried between the hind legs, the tail signals anxiety and uncertainty. In joy the dog wags its tail. A tail carried up expresses greatest excitement and alertness.

Offering a paw: This behavior goes back to the kneading reflex of puppies before the are weaned of their mother's milk. While they suckle at their mother's nipples, puppies instinctively knead the mammary glands to stimulate the flow of milk. When the growing pup tends you its paw, your dog wants to appease you or perhaps invite you to play.

Marking: Dogs mark their territories by leaving their scent mark on trees, posts, and fences. If another dog has perchance left its visiting card already, the dog covers it over with its own

Fetching is one of the favorite occupations of the mountain dog breeds.

scent note. This ritual strengthens its self-confidence. Females don't mark, as a rule, because they don't control their own territories.

Digging and burying: Most dogs blissfully bury a bone somewhere in the yard and then dig it up again sometime later. This behavior pattern is a legacy from their wolf ancestors.

Digging is fun, too.

HOW-TO:
Puppy Language

Although a puppy already knows the entire repertoire of sound or body language, just what it is trying to communicate won't always be clear to the human observer, mainly because the puppy's coordination and body control are still immature.

1) "I have to go" is the meaning of this somewhat uncertain posture.

"I have to go"

Drawing 1

Every puppy behaves differently when it badly needs to go out. Typical behaviors are:
• It sits down more often.
• It runs around excitedly, at the same time sniffing around with its nose to the floor.
• It turns in circles, as if it's trying to bite its tail.
• It already knows the way to

the outside, perhaps stands at the door and looks at you pleadingly.
• It repeatedly bumps you with its nose.

Nose contact

Drawing 2

Puppies blissfully bump "their" people with their noses and lick them, preferably in the face— assuming it's in tongue's reach. This is how the dog expresses affection and tenderness. Jumping in greeting belongs in this same category; it's born of the longing to be as close as possible to the upright-walking two-legs. Puppies who, despite all their skill at jumping, scarcely reach over the human knee often nibble tenderly on shoes, socks, and—failing those—even on naked feet. All told, the puppy uses its nose more often for communication purposes than the adult dog does. A nose bump has various meanings according to the situation: one demands filling its dish, another the necessary march through the front door, the third the overdue petting session.

2) The puppy wants to express its love for you when it nudges you with its nose.

Invitation to Play

Puppies play with each other all day long until they almost collapse with weariness. You're the playmate for your little mountain dog, and your pet needs play just as much as it needs its puppy food. Your puppy summons you to playtime this way:
• Light barking with head upheld, eagerly shining eyes, dancing legs, and joyously wagging tail. Typically, the adult dog invites play with its front legs kept on the floor while the rear end is raised. Puppies usually haven't got this posture down completely, however.
• Growling while watching a toy. A puppy can also growl quite impressively if someone comes near its ball or its chewing bone. Your puppy protects it with a foot or its body. If your pet then lifts its head expectantly, however, it means "Just try to take it away from me!" If you let the growling drive you away, the little one sits there clearly frustrated. Growling is also often accompanied by wild chasing through the living room. The

3) Pressing flat on the floor and looking guilty will move any dog owner.

young dog circles its playmate in the hope that it'll soon play along. If nothing happens, it stops and barks loudly with unmistakable disappointment.

Note: Young dogs of all the four mountain dog breeds are downright fiends for play.

Guilt Without Remorse

There's almost no curbing puppies in their curiosity. With every new experience they become more self-confident. The limits of their journeys of discovery through house and yard should, however, be pointed out to them early on. Otherwise the puppy will soon be dancing on the dining room table. Moreover, a young dog knows very well what it may and may not do. But only too often the forbidden is exciting. If you catch the villain in the act, it appears full of regret and humility.

Drawing 3

Guiltily, the puppy presses flat on the floor and tries to make itself as small as possible, as if it weren't even there. Or it assumes a subservient position, on its side or its back with its tail tucked under and gaze averted. Who can withstand such a moving exhibit of guilt? But you'd better! For you've scarcely turned your back on the dear little thing and the good-for-nothing is already on the way to new crimes. Your puppy has finally mastered perfectly the trick of making you merciful.

When Puppies Whine

Drawing 4

No dog likes to be left alone. An abandoned puppy achieves quick success with whining and whimpering. Hardly anyone, whether another dog or a human being, can shut out those penetrating howls of grief. The idea that a puppy cry of need automatically initiates a rescue mission from older dogs can easily be tested. Simply begin a wail in a higher tone than the one that's going on: Your dog will be reassuringly on the spot in a second.

In the days after its arrival, you've paid tribute to the little fellow's grief at separation. Because of that your puppy was allowed to sleep by your bed, because of that you had eyes and ears only for your pet. But watch out! Careful attempts at training are highly recommended, even at preschool age. Let your pet whimper quietly for a long time once in a while. After a while it will register very clearly that its puppy world still turns if no one rushes to reassure it. Otherwise you'll be raising a world-class whiner.

4) When a puppy thinks it has been left alone, you may hear a heartbreaking wail.

Taking the Puppy Seriously

Whether your young dog bares its teeth aggressively, begs for attention with raised paw, or barks vigilantly—respond to its language just as appropriately as you would for the adult dog in the specific situation. The dog needs the feedback as a sign that it has behaved properly or wrong.

31

Training and Exercise

The four Swiss breeds are all equally above average in their alertness, eagerness to learn, and independent action in a situation.

Training Should Be Fun

Proper training is the real recipe for success in turning the young dog into the happy and reliable partner that every dog owner wants.

1. Make use of your dog's natural behavior patterns.

2. Be consistent but gentle. Commands and obedience are the basis for a conflict-free coexistence. You'll never achieve that goal with hitting.

3. Don't demand too much of the dog in your lessons; stop and rest every once in a while.

Achieving Success Step by Step

• Practice with your dog daily, but only as long as your pet remains enthusiastic about the task.

• Consistency and repetition of the exercises ensure reaching the goal of the training.

• Praise and stroke your dog as soon as it's done something right.

• Only begin with the next practice session when the last training point is reliably established.

• Make your wants clear to the young dog through simple words and gestures. Always use the same ones. It's not the loudness of your voice but the tone alone that's decisive.

You can't begin early enough to train the puppy. If you neglect it, you'll have a dog with all kinds of bad habits later.

The Training Calendar

You can begin to train the puppy to be housebroken as soon as it comes into the house (see page 24).

At the age of three months the young dog learns to connect an instruction with a particular situation. Deliberately playful, you can begin with the preparations for walking on a lead and with the commands "come" and "fetch" (see HOW-TO, pages 34 and 35).

Between four months and eight months issue the commands "speak," "stay," "sit," "heel," and "lie down." Make use of the times of day when the young dog seems especially alert and ready to respond.

What the Mountain Dog May Not Do

1. A mountain dog herds everyone and everything. Keep your pet on the lead while children are running past. If your dog behaves quietly, it should be praised and rewarded.

2. Your pet barks at the least provocation. Withhold a treat from the dog until it barks with eagerness. Then give it the treat with the command "Speak." For inappropriate barking, say "Enough."

3. Your pet takes its role as protector too seriously. Visitors are only reluctantly tolerated, and your dog even rushes after a guest who turns his back to leave. Clearly admonish the dog at every instance, at the same time shaking your pet by the loose skin at the nape of the neck.

The Swissy, like the other three breeds, needs firm but gentle training.

4. Your pet jumps on everyone to express its affection, don't punish it. Instead crouch down, hold it off a little distance (so it can't lick you), praise and stroke your pet.

5. Your pet begs at the table. Remain firm, in spite of those sweet, longing dog eyes.

6. Your pet grips people on the leg who come riding up. Try to stop the tipping with a sharp "No." Put the dog on the lead after each instance and ignore it for a while.

7. Your pet suddenly starts leaving a mess, most likely protesting against something. Pinpoint the problem and if possible, eliminate it.

Warning: Incontinence may be a sign of kidney or intestinal disease.

If you believe that the problem is not caused by illness, begin eliminating this behavior by placing treats or customary feed bowls on the soiled spot.

Training doesn't mean total submission or the perfect precision of the performing animal. Rather, the dog should—indeed must—have the opportunity to freely develop its personality; only then will your pet become the agreeable, well-balanced companion you want.

Collar and Lead

Drawing 1 and 2

Without the help of a lead you can't attempt to go out on the street with a young, disobedient dog. The lead thus gives your pet and you a free space in common.

Ability to walk on a lead begins with the collar. At first you try the unfamiliar collar around your pet's neck rather playfully. If the dog resists, don't make an issue out of it. Don't scold but stroke your pet and repeat the procedure several times a day. Getting used to the leash itself succeeds in familiar

1) Walking on a lead should be practiced. Important: Keep the lead slack!

surroundings, in the yard and in the house. Only when you've established acceptance do you try short walks. Keep the lead loose. Never tug! If your dog tugs on the other end, pull your pet back with a firm pull. Then loosen the leash again at once. Do it as often as necessary until the dog realizes that only staying back is comfortable.

"Sit"

Drawing 3

This involves sitting on command and only getting up again when the order is lifted with "Come." It's part of the basic training of any family dog. To achieve it, hold the standing dog with one hand on the collar or on the lead. With the other hand, gently but firmly press down your pet's rear end until the dog is sitting. Give the command to "Sit" as you perform the action. When it remains sitting obediently, praise your pet.

"Lie Down" and "Stay"

At "Lie down" and "Stay" the dog should sit or lie down while you walk away. It may not follow you until you allow it up again with the order "Come." Everyday life with a family dog is unimaginable without reliable obedience to these commands, whether the family wants to have meals without disturbance or leave the dog waiting patiently outside the grocery store.

For the first attempt, choose a place in which the dog likes to lie down, preferably its bed. Then practice the command "Lie down" and at the same time give the command "Stay" while you slowly move away. Underscore

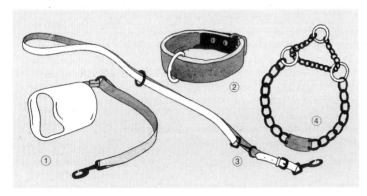

2) The young dog is taken walking with a roll-up lead ① and leather collar ②. The adult dog needs a stout leather leash ③. The choke collar with a stop ring ④ can be used as a training aid for a growing dog.

3) Practicing "Sit": press down gently on the dog's rump while gently pulling the leash up.

your commands with unambiguous gestures. Hold the palm of your hand in front of its muzzle to make it clear to your pet not to follow. Also, as you go away, always show the dog your raised hand (palm). Lift the order with "Come." Only now should you praise your pet for obediently holding out! This exercise is difficult and the dog won't be able to learn it overnight.

"No" and "Stop"

The young dog should learn to quit a particular behavior at the command "No" or "Stop." Thus you deprive it of pleasure in the misbehavior with reproach. Basically, then, you only scold your pet when you catch it in the act. Halt the dog with a loud "No" or "Stop." Underscore the effect with a firm shake of the loose skin at the back of its neck.

The young dog knows this from its mother, who controlled the puppy with a good bite. If you want to take something out of its mouth, hold its nose gently and firmly and lightly press its lips against its teeth. As you do so, give the command "No" or "Stop." When it lets the object fall, reward your pet with stroking.

Coming When Called Is Life Insurance

A dog that runs free must come when it's called! You use the dog's pack instinct to train it to come. Make the first attempts on a field or in a meadow far away from traffic and people. Forgetful of everything, your young dog is completely absorbed with the wonderful new smells around it. Meanwhile, without your pet noticing, you go 10 or 20 yards in the opposite direction. Then you call the dog. With very young dogs, especially, the fear of being left alone overcomes curiosity, The dog comes at a flying gallop.

Important: Praise your pet. Even more—caress and cuddle it.

The dog must treasure its coming to the call as an absolutely wonderful experience.

You can even strengthen your dog's feeling of aloneness the next time with the exercise "Sit." When you're standing far away from your pet, make yourself small by going down on your knees. For the dog, its master or mistress now seems much farther away. The fear of being alone will be overpowering.

Most frequent basic faults of the exercise:
• Repeated calls while the dog runs away and you pant after it. In this case you're only an uncomfortable, annoying sound.
• Reproach and punishment. The dog attaches a negative experience to its return and the next time ignores your command out of sheer anxiety.

4) The commands "Lie down" and "Stay" require the dog to remain standing or lying while you walk away. Reinforce the command by holding up the palm of your hand in front of its nose.

Pulling carts is a passion for the Bernese. The one already harnessed waits impatiently until...

Mountain Dogs Need Work

The mountain dog's inexhaustible will to work is one of its most outstanding character traits. Unfortunately most mountain dogs, as family dogs, are often underchallenged when it comes to work assignments. They are then bored or they can also develop into unstable troublemakers. Here are some suggestions for a suitable activity program for your dog.

Duty: Daily Walks

Even if you have a large yard, it's not enough just to let the dog run there several hours a day. Your mountain dog needs daily walks (see The World Through the Nose, page 28).

How often and how long should you walk? Go walking with your dog at least once a day for an hour. What's good for the dog will also be good for your own health, as you'll discover.

Give the Dog Jobs

You can challenge your mountain dog in a yard or in an open field:

Fetching: It's one of the favorite activities of all four Swiss mountain dog breeds. You throw a piece of wood or a rubber toy (see page 26) far away and give the dog the command to "Fetch." Arrange it so that the dog has to jump over an obstacle—a downed treed trunk, for example, to get the block of wood.

Tracking: All their lives mountain dogs love to follow scents. Two people are needed for this game. One keeps the dog on the lead while the other person runs ahead and hides behind a tree trunk, bush, or building about 30 yards off. The tracking lesson can begin with the command "Find." To keep the game from being too hard at the beginning, you should "garnish" the track with some treats so the dog can follow the scent more easily. When it seeks out the hidden person, it's praised extensively and stroked. Otherwise you can have your mountain dog trained as a tracking dog in a breed club.

Harnessing to a small cart: Serving as draft animals is the special passion of the Bernese and the Swissy. There are special dog carts (see Useful Addresses, page 62) or even a simple slatted wagon to which you can harness your dog. Harnesses must fit the anatomic bone configuration of your mountain dog. Do not make your own harness (see Useful Addresses, page 62). A child can sit in the cart and will certainly love traveling this way. However, you must lead the dog as it pulls the cart.

Guard Duty: Guarding is in the mountain dog's blood. Whether the object is a market basket, bicycle, or car—a guard can be very useful. For basic practice, the dog is attached to a long lead and is commanded to "Stay"

finally the second Bernese is ready and...

they can get going—with milk to the cheesery.

near a familiar object, a jacket, a shoe, or the fetching stick. Give it the command "Watch." Now a helper tries unobtrusively to take away the guarded object. If the dog tries to defend its object and at the same time barks, it's greatly praised. You can quietly repeat this practice many times.

Mountain Dogs Enjoy Trials

If you want to enter your dog in obedience trials, you should turn to the particular breed club (see Useful

Addresses, page 62). You can get the addresses of the appropriate local group from the secretaries of the respective breeder clubs and from the AKC. They'll send you the exact regulations and requirements for the various trials.

Mountain dogs have distinguished themselves in the guarding, tracking, endurance, and companion dog trials. Some have even been used as rescue dogs in avalanches and other catastrophic situations. The comparatively small number used is less an indication of suitability of the possible candidates than it is of the high requirements established by the leaders of rescue dog operations.

Agility

Both humans and dogs are challenged by agility races, a new type of sport from England.

The dog has to run an obstacle course while its owner runs along beside it. Obstacles can be hurdles the dog has to jump over, stakes that must be negotiated in slalom, seesaws the dog must cross, tunnels of material that it must crawl through, or beams on which it must "balance."

In agility races the dog is entered with its owner. In a race, the obstacles must be overcome in a stated time and in an order that is announced shortly before the beginning of the race. Today agility shows are mostly organized supraregionally, some indoors and some outdoors. You can get information and dates from all clubs of dog breeds that are suited to this new kind of sport. However, agility trials are also open to mixed breeds.

Draft Dog Trials

Here more than anywhere else, the Bernese and the Swissy mountain dogs are in their very own element. In Switzerland and in Sweden, the draft dog trials have a special course all to themselves. The dogs' enthusiasm is nearly uncontrollable. During harnessing and before the start, the owners have their hands full to keep the eager draft dogs from crossing the starting line too soon. Even without your own dog participating, a draft dog competition is always worth a visit, if only to see the beautiful hand-worked harnesses and the lovingly prepared dog carts. For information on locations and dates of events, contact the breeder clubs of the Bernese and the Swissy. (see Useful Addresses, page 62). Carts and harnesses are exhibited also at these "freight pulling" shows.

Search and Rescue Trials

All four mountain dog breeds are eager students for search and rescue training. Bernese and Swissies have recently begun to receive invitations to participate in these trials. They are sure to increase in popularity as soon as the registration process moves ahead to full recognition.

The Bernese rolls happily in the dirt. Its coat will need a total bath to get clean again.

Routine Care and Grooming

A showpiece like the Swiss mountain dog, with its marvelous coat, needs regular grooming. For one thing, grooming is more important for maintaining health than it is for cosmetic reasons, and for another, this intensive interaction with each other deepens the bond between owner and dog.

Getting Used to Grooming

Grooming doesn't just mean brushing the dog's coat. There's more to it: inspecting teeth, cleaning ears, removing eye discharges, grooming paws, occasional baths, and also removing a tick once in a while (see page 43). Dogs will often disappear if they suspect that a cleaning or beauty session is about to take place. Thus grooming and letting itself be groomed must be learned, so that the ritual doesn't turn into a joyless program of duties but, rather, an agreeable experience for both parties.

Early acquaintance with a comb and brush is almost as important for the puppy as the very first obedience exercises. Standing still, staying, lying down: If you practice these things with your pet regularly, you'll have no problems with grooming later.

Note: On HOW-TO pages 42 and 43 you will find exact directions for the most important holds during dog grooming.

Monitoring for Signs of Illness

During grooming you can keep an eye out for signs of ill health. Along with regular immunization shots this is the best way to keep your animal healthy (see page 50).

Coat: Dull, dry fur can indicate nutritional deficiencies (see Nutrition, page 44). **Caution:** Before shedding in spring and in late fall, the fur always loses its gloss; it's normal.

Skin: Scaliness and sloughing scabs, usually seen with broken hairs, are indications of incorrect feeding (see Nutrition, page 44).

Teeth: Yellowing means tartar. It is produced primarily by lack of firm food (remedy: gnawing bones, see page 46), but to some degree it's also characteristic of the breed. Tartar is removed by the veterinarian.

Gums: Pale color, an external sign of anemia, is a symptom of various disorders.

Mouth odor: A dog can have bad breath, depending on the composition of its food. If a strong odor doesn't abate after several days and even after a change of diet, it can indicate gastrointestinal problems.

Eyes: Tired eyes are always an alarm signal. As a rule the dog will clearly exhibit changed behavior at the same time. Production of slight discharges is harmless and can be handled by simply wiping them away (see HOW-TO, page 42). In the case of productive secretion and visible conjunctival inflammation, however, the patient should be under a veterinarian's care.

Ears: Regularly use your eyes and nose to inspect your mountain dog's hanging ears. A bad smell usually indicates ear mites.

Daily coat care is foremost among all the important grooming procedures. Long fur like that of the Bernese must be combed and brushed thoroughly so the hair won't tangle. If snarls do form, you can carefully untangle them by hand.

Grooming the coat is part of the daily program, even for puppies.

Paws: If the pad is very brittle, cracks (danger of infection) can result. Look for foreign bodies between the toes. Also, always check the length of the toenails (see HOW-TO, page 42).

Important: See your veterinarian right away at any suspicion of illness.

Keeping Grooming to a Minimum

You can see to it that the grooming program doesn't get extended unnecessarily, especially on walks with your mountain dog.

• Avoid paths with pebbles, for the small and—depending on the type of pebble—sharp little stones can get between the dog's toes and must then be removed (see HOW-TO, page 42).

• In summer, avoid asphalt streets. Great heat often softens the road tar.

The result: Clumps of tar adhere to the hair between the pads of the feet, which must then be cut out.

• During the major tick seasons in late spring and summer, avoid shrubbery and underbrush. Keep the dog on the lead on woodsy paths (see HOW-TO, page 43).

• In winter, in ice and snow, rub the pads of the dog's feet with petroleum jelly before going for a walk. The greasy protective layer prevents foot damage from salt or ice splinters.

Working with the puppy promotes bonding with its owner.

Bathing in Moderation

All four mountain dog breeds are water crazy. They can hardly pass a pond without taking a swim. Nevertheless, they mostly don't care for the total bath in the bathtub at home. A careful showering off may do for them. However, no mountain dog needs a regular shower; twice yearly is all that's necessary for a healthy dog with otherwise regular coat grooming (see HOW-TO, page 43).

Shower and bathing should be prohibited for puppies up to six months old, sick and just-immunized animals, animals with skin problems or wounds, and for pregnant bitches.

How to shower successfully: Lay a rubber mat in the bathtub so that the dog won't slide and the enamel of the bathtub will also be protected. Place the dog in the tub. Check the water temperature. A temperature of about 93°F (about 34°C) (warm to the hand) is ideal. Then, using a hand-held shower attachment, carefully rinse the dog from the legs upward. Avoid the head region, at most slightly dampening the ear and eye areas. Often a partial shower is enough to take care of the dirt-catching rear end. Use a nonalkaline shampoo for dogs (available at your pet store) and make only one application per bath. Afterward rub the dog down vigorously with a towel. A drier dries out the hair too much and frightens many animals. Fur and skin need at least two hours to dry (in a draft-free place).

Alternative to water: Consider dry shampoo with massage liquid or special powder (from the pet store).

HOW-TO:
Grooming

Grooming strengthens the dog's resistance to disease, protects it from wind and weather, and provides your pet with a sense of well-being.

1) Rubbing the teeth with a damp cloth is part of teeth care.

Teeth Care

Drawing 1

Tartar can lead to inflammation of the gums and ultimately to loss of teeth.

A healthy diet avoids the development of tartar. Along with soft food, the dog needs something to bite and gnaw on, for instance a buffalo hide bone or a piece of cowhide (see page 46).

Regularly wiping the teeth down with a damp cloth is also preventive. But if the tartar has already built up a hard deposit, it must be removed by the veterinarian with a special instrument and under anesthesia.

Care of the Paws

Drawing 2

Dry and cracked pads should be rubbed with petroleum jelly. The grease improves elasticity and in winter protects from the destructive effects of salt.

Between the toes small stones and sticks can become embedded—often promoted by long bunches of hair. First clip the hair between the toes to the level of the pads. Then carefully remove the foreign bodies from between the toes or even in the pad itself with the fingers or with tweezers.

Toenails are shortened weekly with a nail file (from the pet store) for puppies. With normally active, alert animals, toenails wear down through running on various different surfaces. At first let the veterinarian show you how to clip toenails so that you don't by mistake cut into the part of the nail that carries blood vessels.

2) Remove stones wedged between the toes with your fingers or tweezers.

Care of Eyes and Ears

Drawings 3 and 4

The brief, daily inspection of eyes and ears is part of the regular grooming program.

Ears: Lift the ears and remove the dirt particles from the underside of the ear with a damp cloth. About every two weeks carefully instill several drops of cleaning oil (from the druggist) into the ear shell. It loosens ear wax and dirt. With the help of a tissue twisted to a point, polish out the ear.

Note: With a heavy ear discharge or smell (ear mites), go to the veterinarian. Frequently scratching at the ear and shaking the head can indicate a foreign body in the inner ear.

Caution: Never clean the inner ear with a cotton-tipped swab (danger of injury). Because of the anatomic features of the dog ear (twisted auditory canal), let the veterinarian show you how to inspect the ears.

Eyes: During sleep, secretions often form in the corners of the dog's eyes. Remove them carefully with a tissue. If you think there's too much discharge, consult the veterinarian.

Inspect the conjunctiva (especially with Bernese) for reddening or inflammation. If you see any, the veterinarian can help.

Accessories for Coat Grooming

Drawing 5

• A coarse steel comb, a flea comb, and a natural-bristle hairbrush with long bristles are recommended for the Bernese.

- For Appenzellers, Entlebuchers, and Swissies, you need a fine-tooth steel comb (flea comb), a brush with short natural bristles, or a rubber curry brush.

Note: Choose only steel combs with rounded teeth.

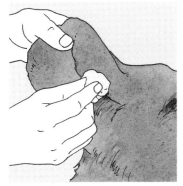

3) Clean the ears with a tissue twisted to a point.

Coat Care

Place the dog on a rubber mat while brushing (because of the danger of sliding).

Bernese: Comb and brush its long coat daily, first with a coarse-tooth steel comb. Carefully loosen snarls by hand. Go over your pet again with a fine-tooth comb (flea comb). Remove all loose hairs with a brush with long, natural bristles—beginning against the grain on the underparts. Then brush the coat with the grain. This provides gloss. A damp chamois removes loose hair and dust particles. Time required is about 15 minutes, somewhat more during shedding season.

Appenzeller, Entlebucher, Swissy: Work over the coat daily with the fine-tooth flea comb. Then remove dead hairs with the natural (short) bristle brush or the rubber curry brush. During shedding season (spring, fall), run

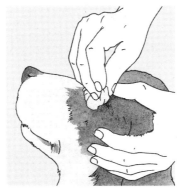

4) Carefully remove secretions from the corners of the eyes with a tissue.

your hand over the coat against the grain daily to remove shedding hairs from the undercoat.

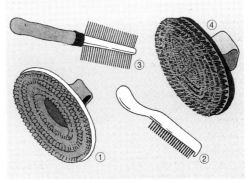

5) Grooming utensils for all mountain dog breeds at a glance. ① rubber curry brush, ② coarse-tooth metal comb, ③ flea comb, ④ brush with natural bristles.

Help with Parasites

Fleas can be picked up by a dog anywhere. Combing with the flea comb frees it of parasites. Sometimes, however, the fleas spread massively and must be combatted because they can cause eczema and they serve as an intermediate host for tapeworms. You can get effective medications from the pet store or your veterinarian (follow instructions carefully!).

Tick season is from late spring to late summer. Ticks sit in bushes or on blades of grass and drop onto humans or animals when brushed. With their proboscis they bore into the skin and suck blood. Ticks can infect humans and animals with diseases and must therefore be removed. During these months, inspect your dog after each walk, particularly its head and chest. Ticks have a dark gray to yellowish gray body that can reach the size of a pea. Grasp the tick with tweezers or a special tick forceps (available at your pet store) and draw it out counterclockwise.

Nutrition

Providing a proper diet for your dog isn't just a matter of giving it enough food but also a well-balanced combination of nutrients, so that your pet stays healthy and fit.

What Dogs Need

A mountain dog likes peace and quiet while eating. Always feed in the same place, where your pet is undisturbed and at regular feeding times.

The wolf, the ancestor of the dog, swallows its quarry—primarily plant-eaters—whole. In so doing, it takes in the undigested plant materials along with the prey animal. Thus its body is provided with the necessary roughage, carbohydrates, minerals such as calcium and phosphorous, and vitamins. Appropriate dog food must contain all these elements, but a diet that is exclusively meat does not provide sufficient quantities. Deficiency symptoms are only the more harmless consequences of such a one-sided diet.

Commercially Prepared Food

This complete diet contains all the nutrients and building blocks that are important for the dog. There is a broad product assortment available—puppy food, low-irritant bland diets, diet programs for overweight animals, and food for old animals—in various forms.

Moist food has a water content of 75 percent and is supplied in cans. You can read the contents on the can label. Anyone who uses mainly canned food should also use dog kibble or cereal—e.g., vegetable flakes—mixed in (two-thirds canned food, one-third flakes) or the dog may get diarrhea.

Semimoist and dry food contain only 10 to 30 percent water and are therefore more concentrated and contain more energy than canned food. If you use this food, your dog needs plenty of fresh drinking water.

My tip: Dry food that has been soaked in unsalted vegetable or fish broth instead of water tastes better to the dog.

Home-prepared Food

To prepare a balanced diet for your mountain dog yourself, you need some basic knowledge about the dog's requirements for nutrients and their utilization.

The protein portion should be between 25 and 50 percent. Protein is found primarily in meat, fish, or cottage cheese. You should always feed cooked meat and fish. Suitable types are: lean muscle meat of beef, veal, horse, or game and chicken. Although not too often (because they're heavily burdened with harmful substances), the dog can have organ meats such as stomach, liver, kidneys, and heart. With fish, it's best to use filet with all bones removed.

Important: Raw pork can carry toxoplasmosis and also Aujeszky's disease (pseudorabies). Raw chicken can carry salmonella!

The carbohydrate portion should make up 45 percent maximum. Carbohydrates are contained in cereals (oat and wheat flakes), potatoes, dog kibble, rice, corn, but also in flour products like noodles and bread. Cereals, rice, noodles, and potatoes should be cooked before feeding.

This splendid-looking mountain dog clearly is fed a well-balanced diet.

The fat portion should not drop below the 5 percent line. Fat provides the body with its main source of energy. Fat is partly contained in meat. Basically you should mix about 2 tablespoons of cold-pressed vegetable oil (for example, wheat-germ oil) into a home-prepared dog meal.

Minerals, trace elements, and vitamins must be added. You can get the appropriate vitamin and mineral mixtures at the pet store and from the veterinarian.

Note: Dog kibble already has vitamins added. If the dog's menu contains kibble, you needn't mix in any additional vitamins and minerals.

The average daily requirement for an adult mountain dog lies somewhere between 10.5 to 14 ounces (300–400 g) of protein, 5.25 to 7 ounces (150–200 g) of carbohydrate, 2 tablespoons of oil, and the vitamin and mineral mixture (used according to directions).

Rules for Feeding

- The food must be neither too cold nor too hot. Room temperature is right.
- Remove any leftover food after about 30 minutes. It then goes bad, which leads to diarrhea for the dog and attracts flies.
- Opened cans and home-prepared food should be kept in the refrigerator for a maximum of two days.
- Clean the feeding dish thoroughly with hot water after every meal, otherwise dangerous bacteria may develop.
- There must always be fresh water available for the dog so that it can quench its thirst anytime.
- Don't disturb the dog while it is eating or it may react aggressively.

These are bad for the dog:
- Spicy foods, like sausage or leftover pickled things, may damage its kidneys.
- Sweets harm its teeth and make your pet fat.

Preparing the Dog Menus

Mix the cooked ingredients with the other components of the dog menu and you're done.

The Dog Needs Bones

It's important that your dog have something firm to gnaw on for chewing practice. Gnawing bones of buffalo hide and cowhide are good for this purpose. Also there's nothing wrong with round bones (joints) of calf or cow twice a week.

How Much Food?

Normal values for the average daily requirement always refer to the adult, nonpregnant, healthy mountain dog with normal weight who does not work.

The puppy, during its main growth phase (up to 12 months old), needs double the amount of nutrients the grown dog does and thus a double quantity of food. It's recommended that you give the puppy special puppy feed from the pet store. Have the breeder give you some of its usual food. That will make the transition easier.

The pregnant bitch needs a diet that's richer in vitamins and more nutritious than the ordinary diet. The quantity can be doubled. Enrich it with some pollard, calcium preparations, and bonemeal.

The old dog needs a carbohydrate-rich diet (more easily digested). Reduce the meat portion and instead mix in more cereals, rice, or kibble.

Feeding Places and Feeding Times

Food and drinking bowls should always be in the same place. Always feed your dog at the same time so that it can be counted on.

The puppy: Until the age of 12 weeks the puppy receives its food ration divided into four portions throughout the day. Up to the age of six months, feed three times a day; up to 18 months, feed twice a day.

The adult dog: Either divide the dog's food ration into a morning and late-afternoon one or give it the whole amount at about midday.

The pregnant dog: She receives her food ration divided into two to three meals throughout the day—preferably in the morning, middle of the day, and late afternoon.

Drinking Is Important

The best drink for a dog is fresh tap water. It must always be available. Milk is not recommended. It may give the dog diarrhea. Some dogs don't like water and therefore drink too little. Try a milk-and-water mixture (proportions: 50–50). But keep an eye out to be sure this drink doesn't cause diarrhea.

Oh, You Fat Dog!

The figure test shows whether your dog is too fat. Feel for the ribs behind the shoulders along the midline of chest height. If you can't feel them, the dog is too fat.

Being overweight can produce many health problems for mountain dogs including:
• accelerated joint stiffening and joint diseases
• hyperextension, inflammation, and tearing of ligaments
• circulatory problems and heart disease
• skin changes (for instance, increased development of scaly skin)
• increased risks during anesthesia if surgery is required.

Important for Dieting

Before you put an overweight dog on a diet, the veterinarian should examine it to see if obesity may have been triggered organically. He or she will check the thyroid, liver, and kid- neys, and get a determination of glucose values and hormone analysis. If the doctor gives the green light, the diet cure can begin. Most likely to be successful is a reducing diet that fulfills the following requirements:
• easily digestible
• balanced content of basic nutrient requirements
• sufficient satisfaction for the animal despite the diminished caloric content
• tastiness.

Split Diet for the Dog

A diet must be effective and tasty. Why not a split diet? That is, exclusive feeding with protein, say meat. Turkey meat without fat is recommended. A vitamin and mineral mixture is added and all other food is taboo! A 14-day cure is reasonable.

Important: Over a long period, feeding just meat can lead to intestinal and digestive problems. Before beginning a diet, consult with your veterinarian to work out a diet program for your dog. There are special diet products available from the veterinarian and from the pet store.

Fat mountain dogs are much more susceptible to illness than dogs with normal weight.

The four Swiss mountain dog breeds are absolutely crazy about children. A small child can grow up completely secure under the protection of a Bernese or a Swissy. A mountain dog is both a playmate and partner for the child, as well as a teacher. The child learns to be responsible and independent.

Health Care

Your mountain dog is not immune to disease, in spite of your best efforts. Keep your eyes peeled for behavioral and bodily conditions in your puppy. Only this way can disease be recognized early. Plan to make one to two visits to your veterinarian yearly, even if your dog isn't sick.

Immunization Shots Are Vital

There are five serious infectious diseases that can especially endanger the life of your dog: rabies, distemper, hepatitis, parvovirus, and leptospirosis. They are transmitted by viruses (except for leptospirosis, which is caused by bacteria) with which the dog can come in contact almost everywhere. The dog can be immunized against all five infectious agents.

Caution: Rabies and leptospirosis are also transmissible to humans (see Important Note, page 63).

If your mountain dog leaves its full dish of food untouched, it could be a sign that your pet is sick.

But an inoculation offers complete protection only if it is renewed regularly. The shots are entered on an immunization card that is given you when you buy the dog from the breeder. You can also use it to figure out the dates for future booster shots.

Note: You can find out the immunization requirements for taking your dog on trips to other countries either from the appropriate consulate or from your veterinarian.

Just as Important: Worming

Internal parasites such as roundworm, tapeworm, or heartworm weaken your dog's resistance. Therefore the dog must be wormed regularly from puppyhood on, for the first time at about four weeks, then again at six and at eight weeks. Ask the breeder whether your puppy has had any or several worm treatments.

Take the information about prior worming treatments by the breeder along with breeder's vaccination records to your veterinarian when you first bring home your new puppy or adult dog.

Depending on the dates and types of treatments an immunizations that have been administered previously, and depending on the geographical area where you live and where the dog will be exposed to outdoor conditions, your veterinarian will select specific medications as well as specific time frames for follow-up treatments.

For example, some rabies vaccines are good up to three years, others need yearly boosters. Most standard viral immunizations require yearly boosters, but many worming treatments require administrations at intervals varying from days to weeks. Never try to treat your dog with over-the-counter worming medication. The treatment of worms is highly specific for each type of parasite. Self help is ill advised and can lead to a very sick dog in your house. Some parasites are endemic in certain regions but not in others, heartworm being the most known. Why endanger your pet with unnecessary medications! Leave the diagnosis and treatment of diseases to your veterinarian and concentrate your efforts on the joys of owning a happy and healthy dog.

Tablets and pastes for worming can be obtained from the veterinarian or by prescription (required for most preparations) at the pharmacy (follow the directions!).

Recognizing the Signs of Illness

Changes in behavior and customary eating habits and digestive disturbances are often the first visible signs of illness. The following checklist should help you to quickly recognize illness in your dog:
• Is your bouncy, lively mountain dog suddenly apathetic? Does your pet sleep much too much?
• Does your dog reject food or water or does it take in more than it usually does?
• Has your pet's stool changed in form or color (diarrhea, eventually with blood and mucus) or does it smell unusual? Is the dog constipated?
• Does your dog have pain when urinating? Is the color of the urine changed?
• Is the coordination of its movements impaired? Does your pet limp?

• Is your dog's coat unkempt and dull? Does the skin show changes (bald spots, scaliness, red spots)? Does it scratch continually?
• Is your dog's nose dry and hot? Are its eyes dull, perhaps inflamed?
• Does your pet still pant after long rest periods?
• Is there a strong odor from your dog's mouth?
• Does your dog have fever or subnormal temperature (see Temperature Taking, HOW-TO, page 54)?

Not every change need be an occasion for worry. But to be sure, you should take the dog to the veterinarian.

Note: When there are changes in stool and urine, always take samples with you!

A Short List of Disease Symptoms

The visible signs of illness described below can have different causes. It's essential to have the veterinarian tell you what you're dealing with.

Coughing: Bronchitis, lung inflammation; heart disease; foreign bodies.

Diarrhea: Excitement, change of diet, worms, infection, poisoning. With a puppy, get to the veterinarian immediately!

Hair loss: Can be caused by various diseases as well as the natural shedding process (related to diet, hormonal problems, metabolic disturbances).

Head shaking: Ear inflammation (mites, bacteria), foreign bodies in the ear.

Heat stroke: The dog is almost unable to move and keeps gasping for air. Among the mountain dogs, the Bernese is especially susceptible to heat.

Poisoning: Various symptoms, depending on the type of poison. At any suspicion, get to the veterinarian at once!

The veterinarian examines the teeth and gums of a young Bernese.

Runny eyes: Inflamed conjunctiva; injury to the cornea; inflammation, injury to the nasolacrimal ducts (tear ducts).

Scratching: Parasites (mites, bacteria), foreign bodies under the skin; skin inflammation caused by fungus (contagious to humans; see Important Note, page 63), allergic causes.

Thirst: Food-related (salty food or dried food); disease-related (disturbance of liver or kidney function, diabetes).

Trembling: Fear; feverish illness.

Vomiting: Dogs can vomit at will in order to relieve themselves. Regular or continuous vomiting: stomach disease, foreign body in stomach, various causes possible. With a puppy, get to the veterinarian at once!

Weight loss: Food deficient in energy; teeth problems (difficulty eating); worms; psychological causes (separation, jealousy); serious illness (tumors).

When the Dog Appears Emotionally Ill

A dog can incur severe psychological stress as a result of frightening experiences (accident shock), serious disappointment, or conflict situations (for example, separation from its family, strife in the family). These negative experiences are often responsible for a multitude of disease pictures, from loss of appetite to massive organic illnesses.

Disorders Specific to the Breeds

There are various reasons for the fact that certain disorders seem to occur especially often in certain breeds.
• In part, dogs are and have been bred for appearance. The attractive exterior counts, while the passing along of defective genes has largely been ignored.
• In part, the gene pool of the breed is so small that inevitably inbreeding problems result.
• In part, genetic diseases often "hide" over several generations so that they can only be discovered with the most modern methods of examination.

Hip dysplasia: In all the large dog breeds and thus also in the Swiss mountain dogs, hip dysplasia (HD) is a typical and common form of disease. In HD, the socket and head of the femur are so severely flattened or loose that painful disturbances of movement result and, in the late stages, lameness as well.

The early diagnosis of the disease is only possible through a radiograph of the pelvis. Today almost all breed clubs connected to the main association (see Useful Addresses, page 62) make a radiograph examination a condition before a dog is permitted to be bred (see Breeding Requirements, page 56).

Elbow dysplasia, osteochondrosis: For mountain dogs, skeletal problems aren't just limited to the hindquarters. In contrast to HD, with its definitive disease picture, elbow dysplasia (ED) and osteochondrosis embrace a broad complex of problems in the region of the shoulder, elbow, knee, and hock. Growth abnormalities in ulna and radius play a role here.

Defects of vision: A hereditary vision defect, progressive retinal atrophy (PRA), can occur, particularly in the Entlebucher. The hereditary, progressive atrophy of the retina can go from night blindness at first through failing visual acuity in the daytime and ultimately to blindness.

Epilepsy: Epilepsy (seizures with convulsions) may sometimes occur in the Swissy.

Histiocytosis: Research has begun on this malignant disease, which has been linked to some of the Bernese mountain dogs. It is suggested that it is transmitted genetically. The breeder organizations in the United States are committed to support research in order to elucidate, diagnose, and finally eliminate this disease. Ask your breeder about any known cases in their dog facilities. Knowledge should not defeat your joy of puppy ownership, but it should be part of your commitment to your new family member.

HOW-TO:
Health

Early recognition of disease, first aid for wounds and accidents, carrying out the veterinarian's instructions—every dog owner can help see to it that his or her pet will quickly become well again.

Temperature Taking

Drawing 1

As a rule, changed behavior of your dog (listless, irritable) is a sign of temperature that is elevated or too low. Feel the lower belly and the inside of the thigh. If these regions are unusually warm, although your dog is not panting, it probably has fever. Contrary to general belief, a hot nose does not indicate fever.

How to Do It: With a dog, it's easier for two people to take the temperature: One holds the standing dog with a hand on the neck and the other hand under the belly, firmly. The other person lifts the dog's tail

high and introduces the thermometer. Use an unbreakable thermometer with digital display. It shows the temperature reliably after 60 seconds. Lubricate the end of the thermometer with petroleum jelly and place it a bit more than 1 inch (about 3 cm) deep into the anus. Hold on to the thermometer while you wait for a reading! If the reading is over or under the normal body temperature of 101.3 to 102.2°F (38.5–39°C), the dog is sick.

Taking the Dog to the Veterinarian

It's important that you give the veterinarian as exact information as possible for the diagnosis and treatment of your sick dog.
• Make notes of all observations that could be important for the history of the illness.
• In the case of changes in stools and urine, take samples with you.
• If the dog has already been receiving medications that were not prescribed by this veterinarian, note the names or take the package with you.

• Don't forget the immunization card!
Transport to the veterinarian is best managed by car. A second person should sit in the backseat with the animal on the trip. Lay a cover over the patient as a protection against chills.

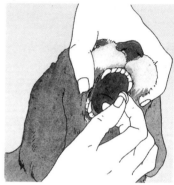

2) Place a pill deep in the throat and briefly hold the muzzle closed so that the dog will swallow it.

Administering Medications

Drawing 2

Conceal a pill cunningly in a little ball of meat? Or mix it in under a pile of food? Most dogs know these tricks and spit it all out again. The only thing left is "the hard way." Open the dog's mouth (with firm pressure behind the jaw region) and lay the pill as far back in the throat as possible. Press the chin upward and briefly hold the jaws closed. The patient will swallow its medicine automatically.

Liquid medications are sprayed with a plastic syringe without a needle (obtained at a

1) It is better to have two people to take a dog's temperature. One person holds the dog firmly around the neck and under the belly while the other lifts the tail and inserts the thermometer in the anus.

pharmacy) through the teeth at the side in small amounts. Carefully pull the flews of the dog up with the fingers of one hand and at the same time hold the dog's head slightly up.

Eye salves are laid under the upper lid in a "string." Lift the lid gently and apply.

Eyedrops are dripped behind the lower lid. Gently pull the lid down.

A Small Household First Aid Kit

For treatment and bandaging of small wounds, but also for prevention, it's a good idea to have a small household first aid kit just for your dog. Keep everything separate from your own first aid kit, of course!

Instruments: Unbreakable digital thermometer, tick forceps, wooden spatula or plastic glove for applying salves, bandage scissors, tweezers with rounded tips, plastic syringe without a needle.

Bandaging materials: Elastic-gauze bandages 2.25 and 4 inches (6 and 10 cm) wide, gauze compresses, adhesive tape, sterile cotton, tissues, lint-free cloth.

Medications: Charcoal tablets for diarrhea; worming medication (note the expiration date!); vitamin and mineral mixture; suppositories for pain analgesia, muscle relaxation, and lowering fever.

Salves and drops: Wound salve, petroleum jelly, baby oil (ear cleaning), eyedrops (note the expiration date!).

For disinfection: Alcohol (propanol) for cooling rubs and for disinfection of instruments; materials for wound disinfection.

Treating Wounds and Applying Bandages

Small wounds that need not be bandaged by the veterinarian are cleaned regularly (often several times a day) with a clean gauze pad and then treated with a wound powder or healing salve (from the pharmacy).

Bandages should be changed daily, or as indicated by the veterinarian, depending on the condition of the wound or the foregoing operation. However, use fresh bandages and compresses (available from your pharmacy). Bandages covering a large area that must be worn over an extended time can be secured with a T-shirt cut to fit or pantyhose and thus protected from dirt.

Help for Insect Stings

Insect stings aren't so rare, for the dog strikes or snaps at wasps and bees. And sometimes the stinger of the insect is faster.

As long as the dog shows no allergic reaction (for instance, vomiting, heavy breathing, and coughing fits) and has only been stung in the foot or on the body, you can ease you pet's pain by cooling the affected area with water or ice. Remove the insect sting first, if it's visible. If the insect has stung the dog in the throat area, it can produce dangerous swelling that may produce breathing and swallowing difficulties and, in the worst case, lead to suffocation. Take the dog to the veterinarian immediately.

First Aid for Accidents and Bites

Drawing 3

If your dog is hit by a car or has gotten into a scrape with another dog, it can sustain wounds that bleed heavily. Then you need to practice first aid:

3) In wounds involving a blood vessel, you must apply a pressure bandage immediately.

For heavily bleeding wounds apply a pressure bandage (see Drawing 3). First clean the wound of large foreign bodies. Then fold a compress or clean material into a thick layer and press it on the wound. Wrap the whole thing with gauze bandage or in a scarf. The bandage is properly fixed if you can still slide a finger underneath it without any difficulty. Then drive to the veterinarian at once.

Note: If there's no bandaging material available, use your hand to press on the injured vessel so the dog doesn't bleed to death.

Breeding

The primary purpose in breeding pedigreed dogs is to retain the positive characteristics typical of the breed and, if possible, to improve them. So it's important to breed only healthy mountain dogs with stable temperaments.

The Standard for Purebred Dogs

The standard, established by the breed club, specifies all the desirable body and temperament characteristics of the particular breed.

In Europe, an additional step of breed selection is formally required (see A Short Glossary, page 11): A commission of judges decides the breeding qualifications of a dog by assigning it points for its conformation to the desirable characteristics described in the standard. The commission issues breeding prohibitions, restrictions, and recommendations. In addition, the European Mountain Dog Club requires a list of basic examinations for its potential breeding animals. This type of breeder selection is not required in the United States.

The Swiss Mountain Dog Club of Germany (SSV) has taken important steps to combat the illnesses that are typical of these breeds. It has introduced a certificate of breeding suitability (ZWS), which is based on all the known hip dysplasia assessments of the past ten years (see Hip dysplasia, page 53). Not only does the ZWS take into consideration the individual constitution of a breeding animal but also its genetic inheritance. The breeding cer-

tificates for all the purebred dogs in the breeding area are entered in the annual studbook of the SSV.

Breeder clubs throughout the United States are attempting to improve breeding stock. New guidelines are being developed to help with the elimination of inherited diseases. The national and local breeder clubs will assist you in finding information and help if you intend to breed mountain dogs (see Useful Addresses, page 62).

How Do You Get Dogs for Breeding?

Contact the puppy or dog supplier or the appropriate breed club secretary (see Useful Addresses, page 62). The breed secretary will advise you on all questions having to do with planning to breed except for raising and maintaining the puppies.

Breeding Requirements

Pedigree: Only use a mountain dog with a recognized pedigree for breeding. The forebears are entered on the pedigree. This is important, for they've contributed their genes to the offspring.

Breeding requirements: According to general breeding requirements for purebred mountain dogs, the minimum breeding ages for males and females is 18 months. The maximum age for mating is unlimited for the male, but the bitch may not be older than eight years.

Permission to breed: In Europe, it is a requirement that mountain dogs that are to be bred must be presented at a

It isn't important to your dog's emotional balance whether it has ever bred or had puppies.

Before it's time to go exploring again, there has to be a little rest period.

breeding-examination meeting to the commission that gives the permission to breed. Only dogs with the conformation grades "very good" and "excellent" are given permission to breed. The permission is entered on the pedigree. A list of breeding qualifications gives the information about the evaluation of the mountain dog. It is presented to the owner of the breeding partner at the time of breeding. This requirement is not standard in the United States. However, it can be said that responsible breeders are becoming increasingly vigilant as to the selection of breeder males and females.

The Sire

As a rule owners of a female dog do not have a male dog as well. More often, when it's time to breed, they look for a partner for the female among the dogs of fellow breeders. It's customary to take the female to the male. The owner of the male usually requires a breeding fee.

Sexual Receptivity

Male: The male is ready to mate any time. As soon as there's a female in estrus, he will use any means to get "an invitation."

Female: As a rule the female's first estrus occurs at around eight months. The "season" or "heat," as estrus is also called, lasts for approximately three weeks and occurs in three phases:
• Proestrus (the first 10 days): The vulva swells, the female acts restless. She bleeds slightly. The blood is dark in color. On walks the female deposits more "urine trickles" than usual, to entice the males. She still angrily rejects any attempts to get close.
• Estrus (10 to 16 days): The bloody discharge is now light pink. The bleeding diminishes or stops altogether. The female is receptive.
• Postestrus: It lasts only a few days. The swelling of the vulva goes down; the behavior of the female becomes normal.

Mating should occur on the eleventh day of estrus. To make sure, it should be repeated on the thirteenth day.

Copulation

Copulation can take 30 minutes or more. During copulation the male's penis and the ring-shaped corpus cavernosum at the end of the penis swell, while the female's vaginal ring constricts. The dogs are "tied" together. Do not separate the dogs at this time or serious injuries can result.

Pregnancy

Your mountain dog is pregnant for about 63 days. From the fifth week you can tell that she's getting stouter.

Weigh the puppy regularly (keep a weight record). If the puppy fails to gain weight, a trip to the veterinarian is indicated.

Usually she's also more affectionate now, too. The swelling of the genitalia during estrus has not completely gone down. A slight mucous discharge occurs, and the nipples are enlarged. She's hungrier than usual (see page 46).

False pregnancy produces the same symptoms in the bitch as a true pregnancy (rounder belly, swollen nipples). She finds herself a "substitute baby"— sometimes a stuffed animal—and puts it to her teats, which in fact contain milk. Remove the substitute baby immediately.

The Whelping Box

Equipment: The wooden whelping box (at least 47 by 39 inches and 16 inches high [119 x 99 x 40.6 cm]) is furnished with a thick layer of shredded newspaper on the bottom. This keeps the puppies warm, soaks up the urine, and should be changed daily.

Location: A quiet, draft-free corner is best. Install an infrared warming lamp with a 150-watt bulb about 5 feet (1.5 m) above the whelping box.

The Birth

On the day of the birth, the bitch becomes restless and begins to scratch up a "nest." After the preliminary pains come the final contractions that serve to open the mouth of the uterus. The bitch stands or lies on her side. Fluid issues from the vagina. Shortly after this, the first puppy appears. The bitch frees the puppy from the amniotic sac and the placenta and bites through the umbilical cord. The mother licks the newborn thoroughly all over in order to start the circulation. Stay near the bitch during the pains and the birth so as to be able to intervene immediately if something goes wrong.

Complications: Problems do occur during birth. You should speak to your veterinarian before the due date and

Development of Puppies

Puppies are born with all their fur. Until day 10 their eyes are closed. From day 12 they can hear. Their sense of smell functions from the first. They unerringly find the source of milk, the mother's nipples.

Note: At two weeks, begin decreasing the temperature in the whelping box so the pups adjust to room temperature.

In the first three weeks the young stay close to their mother and sleep a great deal.

At the fourth week they start their first exploratory expeditions.

At six weeks they begin the imprinting phase. They "discover" themselves and their siblings. Now you should spend a lot of time with the puppies to help them develop an open relationship with people.

From the eighth to the twelfth week, the socialization phase, the puppies try out different behaviors by playing with their siblings.

make sure you can summon help if necessary.

Feeding the Puppies

For the first four weeks the mother will nurse the puppies. During this time give her a double quantity of food mixed with calcium. From the fifth week on, you must feed the puppies, preferably with a special diet (see How Much Food? page 46).

Tip: Have the puppies vaccinated and dewormed (see Health Care, page 50).

Showing Mountain Dogs

Firm rules guide participation in breed shows. The most coveted U.S. championship can be reached only through shows authorized by the AKC; worldwide championships, by the Federation Cynologique Internationale. Happily, judgment of behavior has become more important of late.

Eligibility: Purebred dogs with valid registration papers from the AKC. Recommended minimum age: nine months; for the youngest class: six months.

The AKC strictly regulates showing of dogs. Novices are advised to get information early.

For classification, dogs are divided into age groups or groups based on the original purposes of the breeds. Mountain dogs are grouped under "Working Dogs." Each entrant is awarded a conformation score.

The International Best in Show is a dog that has won the International Championship four times. Newcomers begin with shows for their breed. National titles are awarded through AKC-sponsored shows. The point system used in the United States is strictly followed by all dog clubs. The regulations for the various championships are published by the AKC (see Useful Addresses, page 62).

Senior Shows: Increasingly popular, senior shows are for dogs over eight years old. Lively temperament and impeccable health are especially desirable. As a rule, senior show champions come from breeding lines that feature long life and vitality.

Good Citizen Shows: Quickly rising in popularity, good citizen shows are open to all dog breeds, groups, and ages. They measure and reward good behavior with regard to pedigree.

Last But Not Least

Breeding and showing purebred dogs is time-consuming and expensive. If, this is your goal, contact the AKC for all the information, regulations, and forms.

Index

Useful Addresses and Literature

Clubs and Societies

American Kennel Club
Registration services:
5580 Centerview Drive
Raleigh, North Carolina 27606
(919) 233-9767
Other departments:
51 Madison Avenue
New York, New York 10010
(212) 696-8200

Bernese Mountain Dog Club of
America*
Breeder Club Secretary
Roxanne Bortnick
812 Warren Landing
Fort Collins, Colorado 80525

Greater Swiss Mountain Dog Club of
America, Inc.*
Corresponding Secretary
DeAnne Gerner
91 Schoffers Road
Reading, Pennsylvania 19606
(215) 779-9217

*This address may change with the
election of new club officers. The
current listing can be obtained by
contacting the American Kennel
Club.

Dog Carts and Accessories

Dog Works Inc.
R.R. 3, Box 317
Curvin Circle
Stewartstown, Pennsylvania 17363
(800) 787-2788

Liability Insurance

Almost all house/apartment liability
insurers now offer liability insurance for dogs.

Health Insurance

Veterinary Pet Insurance
(DVM/VPI)
4175 La Palma Avenue
Suite 100
Anaheim, California 92807
(714) 996-2311
(800) USA-PETS

Information and Printed Material

American Boarding Kennel
Association
4575 Galley Road, Suite 400 A
Colorado Springs, Colorado 80915
(Publishes lists of approved boarding
kennels.)

American Society for the Prevention
of Cruelty to Animals (ASPCA)
441 East 92nd Street
New York, New York 10128

American Veterinary Medical
Association
930 North Meacham Road
Schaumburg, Illinois 60173

Gaines Dog Food Company
P.O. Box 8172
Kankakee, Illinois 60901
(Publishes *Touring with Towser*, a
directory of hotels and motels that
accommodate guests with dogs.)

Humane Society of the United States
(HSUS)
2100 L Street NW
Washington, DC 20037

Books

In addition to the most recent
edition of the official publication
of the American Kennel Club, *The
Complete Dog Book*, published by
Howell Book House, New York,
other suggestions include:

Alderton, David. *The Dog Care
Manual*. Hauppauge, New York:
Barron's Educational Series, Inc.,
1986.

Baer, Ted. *Communicating with Your
Dog*. Hauppauge, New York:
Barron's Educational Series, Inc.,
1989.

———. *How to Teach Your Old Dog
New Tricks*. Hauppauge, New
York: Barron's Educational Series,
Inc., 1991.

Klever, Ulrich. *The Complete Book
of Dog Care*. Hauppauge, New
York: Barron's Educational Series,
Inc., 1989.

———. *Dogs: A Mini Fact Finder*.
Hauppauge, New York: Barron's
Educational Series, Inc., 1990.

Pinney, Chris C., *Guide to Home Pet
Grooming*. Hauppauge, New York:
Barron's Educational Series, Inc.,
1990.

Streitferdt, Uwe. *Healthy Dog,
Happy Dog*. Hauppauge, New
York: Barron's Educational Series,
Inc., 1994.

What might they get into next?

Ullmann, Hans. *The New Dog Handbook*. Hauppauge, New York: Barron's Educational Series, Inc., 1984.

Wrede, Barbara. *Civilizing Your Puppy*. Hauppauge, New York: Barron's Educational Series, Inc., 1992.

Periodicals

Pure-Bred Dogs/American Kennel Gazette
51 Madison Avenue
New York, New York 10010
(Published by the American Kennel Club)

Videos

American Kennel Club Video Series: Bernese Mountain Dog, #VVT605
5580 Centerview Drive
Suite 200
Raleigh, North Carolina 27606
(919) 233-9780

About the Author

Gerd Ludwig, Ph.D., is a zoologist and freelance journalist. He is also the editor of the periodical *Das Tier (The Animal)*, for which he writes articles about pets and environmental protection.

About the Photographer

Christine Steimer has worked as a freelance photographer since 1985. She has been specializing in animal photography since 1989 and has worked for the periodical *Das Tier.*

All inquiries should be addressed to:
Barron's Educational Series, Inc.
250 Wireless Boulevard
Hauppauge, NY 11788

© Copyright 1995 by Barron's Educational Series, Inc.

International Standard Book No. 0-8120-9135-3

Library of Congress Catalog Card No. 94-49012

Library of Congress Cataloging-in-Publication Data
Ludwig, Gerd.
    [Sennenhunde. English]
    The Bernese and other mountain dogs : Bernese, Greater Swiss, Appenzellers, and Entlebuchers : everything about purchase, care, nutrition, breeding, behavior, and training / Gerd Ludwig, Christine Steimer : drawings by György Jankovics ; translated from the German by Elizabeth D. Crawford.
        p.   cm. — (A complete pet owner's manual)
    Includes bibliographical references (p. 64) and index.
    ISBN 0-8120-9135-3
    1. Bernese mountain dog. I. Steimer, Christine. II. Title. III. Series.
SF429.B47L8313   1995
636.7'3—dc20   94-49012
                                                                        CIP

Printed in Hong Kong

56789   9955   987654321

Important Notes

This pet owner's guide tells the reader how to buy and care for Bernese, Greater Swiss, Appenzeller, and Entlebucher. The author and the publisher consider it important to point out that the advice given in the book is meant primarily for normally developed puppies from a good breeder—that is, dogs of excellent physical health and good character.

Anyone who adopts a fully grown dog should be aware that the animal has already formed its basic impressions of human beings. The new owner should watch the animal carefully, including its behavior toward humans, and should meet the previous owner. If the dog comes from a shelter, it may be possible to get some information on the dog's background and peculiarities there.

There are dogs that, as a result of bad experiences with humans, behave in an unnatural manner or may even bite. Only people that have experience with dogs should take in such animals.

Caution is further advised in the association of children with dogs, in meeting with other dogs, and in exercising the dog without a leash.

Even well-behaved and carefully supervised dogs sometimes do damage to someone else's property or cause accidents. It is therefore in the owner's interest to be adequately insured against such eventualities, and we strongly urge all dog owners to purchase a liability policy that covers their dog.